# To Dogs Peace On Earth, Good-Will

(Eleanor Hallowell Abbott)

**KARTINDO PUBLISING HOUSE (Kartindo.com)**

# CONTENTS

* * * * *

**KARTINDO PUBLISING HOUSE (Kartindo.com)**

# *PART I*

If you don't like Christmas stories, don't read this one!

And if you don't like dogs I don't know just what to advise you to do!

For I warn you perfectly frankly that I am distinctly pro-dog and distinctly pro-Christmas, and would like to bring to this little story whatever whiff of fir-balsam I can cajole from the make-believe forest in my typewriter, and every glitter of tinsel, smudge of toy candle, crackle of wrapping paper, that my particular brand of brain and ink can conjure up on a single keyboard! And very large-sized dogs shall romp through every page! And the mercury shiver perpetually in the vicinity of zero! And every foot of earth be crusty-brown and bare with no white snow at all till the very last moment when you'd just about given up hope! And all the heart of the story is very,--oh *very* young!

For purposes of propriety and general historical authenticity there are of course parents in the story. And one or two other oldish persons. But they all go away just as early in the narrative as I can manage it.--Are obliged to go away!

Yet lest you find in this general combination of circumstances some sinister threat of audacity, let me conventionalize the story at once by opening it at that most conventional of all conventional Christmas-story hours,--the Twilight of Christmas Eve.

Nuff said?--Christmas Eve, you remember? Twilight? Awfully cold weather? And somebody very young?

Now for the story itself!

After five blustering, wintry weeks of village speculation and gossip there was of course considerable satisfaction in being the first to solve the mysterious holiday tenancy of the Rattle-Pane House.

Breathless with excitement Flame Nourice telephoned the news from the village post-office. From a pedestal of boxes fairly bulging with red-wheeled go-carts, one keen young elbow rammed for balance into a gay glassy shelf of stick-candy, green tissue garlands tickling across her cheek, she sped the message to her mother.

"O Mother-Funny!" triumphed Flame. "I've found out who's Christmasing at the Rattle-Pane House!--It's a red-haired setter dog with one black ear! And he's sitting at the front gate this moment! Superintending the unpacking of the furniture van! And I've named him Lopsy!"

"Why, Flame; how--absurd!" gasped her mother. In consideration of the fact that Flame's mother had run all the way from the icy-footed chicken yard to answer the telephone it shows distinctly what stuff she was made of that she gasped nothing else.

And that Flame herself re-telephoned within the half hour to acknowledge her absurdity shows equally distinctly what stuff *she* was made of! It was from the summit of a crate of holly-wreaths that she telephoned this time.

"Oh Mother-Funny," apologized Flame, "you were perfectly right. No lone dog in the world could possibly manage a great spooky place like the Rattle-Pane House. There are two other dogs with him! A great long, narrow sofa-shaped dog upholstered in lemon and white,--something terribly ferocious like 'Russian Wolf Hound' I think he is! But I've named him Beautiful-Lovely! And there's the neatest looking paper-white coach dog just perfectly ruined with ink-spots! Blunder-Blot, I think, will make a good name for him! And--"

"Oh--Fl--ame!" panted her Mother. "Dogs--do--not--take houses!" It was not from the chicken-yard that she had come running this time but only from her Husband's Sermon-Writing-Room in the attic.

"Oh don't they though?" gloated Flame. "Well, they've taken this one, anyway! Taken it by storm, I mean! Scratched all the green paint off the front door! Torn a hole big as a cavern in the Barberry Hedge! Pushed the sun-dial through a bulkhead!--If it snows to-night the cellar'll be a Glacier! And--"

"Dogs--do--not--take--houses," persisted Flame's mother. She was still persisting it indeed when she returned to her husband's study.

Her husband, it seemed, had not noticed her absence. Still poring over the tomes and commentaries incidental to the preparation of his next Sunday's sermon his fine face glowed half frown, half ecstasy, in the December twilight, while close at his elbow all unnoticed a smoking kerosine lamp went smudging its acrid path to the ceiling. Dusky lock for dusky lock, dreamy eye for dreamy eye, smoking lamp for smoking lamp, it might have been a short-haired replica of Flame herself.

"Oh if Flame had only been 'set' like the maternal side of the house!" reasoned Flame's Mother. "Or merely dreamy like her Father! Her Father being only dreamy could sometimes be diverted from his dreams! But to be 'set' and 'dreamy' both? Absolutely 'set' on being absolutely 'dreamy'? That was Flame!" With renewed tenacity Flame's Mother reverted to Truth as Truth. "Dogs do *not* take houses!" she affirmed with unmistakable emphasis.

"Eh? What?" jumped her husband. "Dogs? Dogs? Who said anything about dogs?" With a fretted pucker between his brows he bent to his work again. "You interrupted me," he reproached her. "My sermon is about Hell-Fire.--I had all but smelled it.--It was very disagreeable." With a gesture of impatience he snatched up his notes and tore them in two. "I think I will write about the Garden of Eden instead!" he rallied. "The Garden of Eden in Iris time! Florentina Alba everywhere! Whiteness! Sweetness!--Now let me see,--orris root I believe is deducted from the Florentina Alba--."

"U--m--m--m," sniffed Flame's Mother. With an impulse purely practical she started for the kitchen. "The season happens to be Christmas time," she suggested bluntly. "Now if you could see your way to make a sermon that smelt like doughnuts and plum-pudding--"

"Doughnuts?" queried her Husband and hurried after her. Supplementing the far, remote Glory-of-God expression in his face, the glory-of-doughnuts shone suddenly very warmly.

Flame at least did not have to be reminded about the Seasons.

"Oh *mother*!" telephoned Flame almost at once, "It's--so much nearer Christmas than it was half an hour ago! Are you sure everything will keep? All those big packages that came yesterday? That humpy one especially? Don't you think you ought to peep? Or poke? Just the teeniest, tiniest little peep or poke? It would be a shame if anything spoiled! A--turkey--or a--or a fur coat--or anything."

"I am--making doughnuts," confided her Mother with the faintest possible taint of asperity.

"O--h," conceded Flame. "And Father's watching them? Then I'll hurry! M--Mother?" deprecated the excited young voice. "You are always so horridly right! Lopsy and Beautiful-Lovely and Blunder-Blot are *not* Christmasing all alone in the Rattle-Pane House! There is a man with them! Don't tell Father,--he's so nervous about men!"

"A--man?" stammered her Mother. "Oh I hope not a young man! Where did he come from?"

"Oh I don't think he came at all," confided Flame. It was Flame who was perplexed this time. "He looks to me more like a person who had always been there! Like something I mean that the dogs found in the attic! Quite crumpled he is! And with a red waistcoat!--A--A butler perhaps?--A--A sort of a second hand butler? Oh Mother!--I wish we had a butler!"

"Flame--?" interrupted her Mother quite abruptly. "Where are you doing all this telephoning from? I only gave you eighteen cents and it was to buy cereal with."

"Cereal?" considered Flame. "Oh that's all right," she glowed suddenly. "I've paid cash for the telephoning and charged the cereal."

With a swallow faintly guttural Flame's Mother hung up the receiver. "Dogs--do--not--have--butlers," she persisted unshakenly.

She was perfectly right. They did not, it seemed.

No one was quicker than Flame to acknowledge a mistake. Before five o'clock Flame had added a telephone item to the cereal bill.

"Oh--Mother," questioned Flame. "The little red sweater and Tam that I have on?--Would they be all right, do you think, for me to make a call in? Not a formal call, of course,--just a--a neighborly greeting at the door? It being Christmas Eve and everything!--And as long as I have to pass right by the house anyway?--There is a lady at the Rattle-Pane House! A--A--what Father would call a Lady Maiden!--Miss--"

"Oh not a real lady, I think," protested her Mother. "Not with all those dogs. No real lady I think would have so many dogs.--It--It isn't sanitary."

"Isn't--sanitary?" cried Flame. "Why Mother, they are the most absolutely--perfectly sanitary dogs you ever saw in your life!" Into her eager young voice an expression of ineffable dignity shot suddenly. "Well--really, Mother," she said, "In whatever concerns men or crocheting--I'm perfectly willing to take Father's advice or yours. But after all, I'm eighteen," stiffened the young voice. "And when it comes to dogs--I must use my own judgment!"

"And just what is the lady's name?" questioned her Mother a bit weakly.

"Her name is 'Miss Flora'!" brightened Flame. "The Butler has just gone to the Station to meet her! I heard him telephoning quite frenziedly! I think she must have missed her train or something! It seemed to make everybody very nervous! Maybe *she's* nervous! Maybe she's a nervous invalid! With a lost Lover somewhere! And all sorts of pressed flowers!--Somebody ought to call anyway! Call right away, I mean, before she gets any more nervous!--So many people's first impressions of a place--I've heard--are spoiled for lack of some perfectly silly little thing like a nutmeg grater or a hot water bottle! And oh, Mother, it's been so long since any one lived in the Rattle-Pane House! Not for years and years and years! Not dogs, anyway! Not a lemon and white wolf hound! Not setters! Not spotty dogs!--Oh Mother, just one little wee single minute at the door? Just long enough to say 'The Rev. and Mrs. Flamande Nourice, and Miss Nourice, present their compliments!'--And are you by any chance short a marrow-bone? Or would you possibly care to borrow an extra quilt to rug-up under the kitchen table?... Blunder-Blot doesn't look very thick. Or--Oh Mother, *p-l-e-a-s-e!*"

When Flame said "Please" like that the word was no more, no less, than the fabled bundle of rags or haunch of venison hurled back from a wolf-pursued sleigh to divert the pursuer even temporarily from the main issue. While Flame's Mother paused to consider the particularly flavorous sweetness of that entreaty,--to picture the flashing eye, the pulsing throat, the absurdly crinkled nostril that invariably accompanied all Flame's entreaties, Flame herself was escaping!

Taken all in all, escaping was one of the best things that Flame did.... As well as the most becoming! Whipped into scarlet by the sudden plunge from a stove-heated store into the frosty night her young cheeks fairly blazed their bright reaction. Frost and speed quickened her breath. Glint for glint her shining eyes challenged the moon. Fearful even yet that some tardy admonition might overtake her she sped like a deer through the darkness.

It was a dull-smelling night. Pretty, but very dull-smelling. Disdainfully her nostrils crinkled their disappointment.

"Christmas Time adventures ought to smell like Christmas!" she scolded. "Maybe if I'm ever President," she argued, "I won't do so awfully well with the Tariff or things like that! But Christmas shall smell of Christmas! Not just of frozen mud! And camphor balls!... I'll have great vats of Fir Balsam essence at every street corner! And gigantic atomizers! And every passerby shall be sprayed! And stores! And churches! And--And everybody who doesn't like Christmas shall be *dipped*!"

Under her feet the smoothish village road turned suddenly into the harsh and hobbly ruts of a country lane. With fluctuant blackness against immutable blackness great sweeping pine trees swished weirdly into the horizon. Where the hobbly lane curved darkly into a meadow through a snarl of winter-stricken willows the rattle of a loose window-pane smote quite distinctly on the ear. It was a horrid, deserted sound. And with the instinctive habit of years Flame's little hand clutched at her heart. Then quite abruptly she laughed aloud.

"Oh you can't scare me any more, you gloomy old Rattle-Pane House!" she laughed. "You're not deserted now! People are Christmasing in you! Whether you like it or not you're being Christmased!"

Very tentatively she puckered her lips to a whistle. Almost instantly from the darkness ahead a dog's bark rang out, deep, sonorous, faintly suspicious. With a little chuckle of joy she crawled through the Barberry hedge and emerged for a single instant only at her full height before three furry shapes came hurtling out of the darkness and toppled her over backwards.

"Stop, Beautiful-Lovely!" she gasped. "Stop, Lopsy! Behave yourself, Blunder-Blot! *Sillies*! Don't you know I'm the lady that was talking to you this morning through the picket fence? Don't you know I'm the lady that fed you the box of cereal?--Oh dear--Oh dear--Oh dear," she struggled. "I knew, of course, that there were three dogs--but who ever in the world would have guessed that three could be so many?"

As expeditiously as possible she picked herself up and bolted for the house with two furry shapes leaping largely on either side of her and one cold nose sniffing interrogatively at her heels. Her heart was very light,--her pulses jumping with excitement,--an occasional furry head doming into the palm of her hand warmed the whole bleak night with its sense of mute companionship. But the back of her heels felt certainly very queer. Even the warm yellow lights of the Rattle-Pane House did not altogether dispel her uneasiness.

"Maybe I'd better not plan to make my call so--so very informal," she decided suddenly. "Not at a house where there are quite so many dogs! Not at a house where there is a butler ... anyway!"

Crowding and pushing and yelping and fawning around her, it was the dogs who announced her ultimate arrival. Like a drift of snow the huge wolf-hound whirled his white shagginess into the vestibule. Shrill as a banging blind the impetuous coach-dog lurched his sleek weight against the door. Sucking at a crack of light the red setter's kindled nose glowed and snorted with dragonlike ferocity. Without knock or ring the door-handle creaked and turned, three ecstatic shapes went hurtling through a yellow glare into the hall beyond, and Flame found herself staring up into the blinking, astonished eyes of the crumpled old man with the red waistcoat.

**KARTINDO PUBLISING HOUSE (Kartindo.com)**

"G--Good evening,--Butler!" she rallied.

"Good evening, Miss!" stammered the Butler.

"I've--I've come to call," confided Flame.

"To--call?" stammered the Butler.

"Yes," conceded Flame. "I--I don't happen to have an engraved card with me." Before the continued imperturbability of the old Butler all subterfuge seemed suddenly quite useless. "I *never* have had an engraved card," she confided quite abruptly. "But you might tell Miss Flora if you please--" ... Would nothing crack the Butler's imperturbability?... Well maybe she could prove just a little bit imperturbable herself! "Oh! Butlers don't 'tell' people things, do they?... They always 'announce' things, don't they?... Well, kindly announce to Miss Flora that the--the Minister's Daughter is--at the door!... Oh, *no*! It isn't asking for a subscription or anything!" she hastened quite suddenly to explain. "It's just a Christian call!... B--Being so nervous and lost on the train and everything ... we thought Miss Flora might be glad to know that there were neighbors.... We live so near and everything.... And can run like the wind! Oh, not Mother, of course!... She's a bit stout! And Father starts all right but usually gets thinking of something else! But I...? Kindly announce to Miss Flora," she repeated with palpable crispness, "that the Minister's Daughter is at the door!"

Fixedly old, fixedly crumpled, fixedly imperturbable, the Butler stepped back a single jerky pace and bowed her towards the parlor.

"Now," thrilled Flame, "the adventure really begins."

It certainly was a sad and romantic looking parlor, and strangely furnished, Flame thought, for even "moving times." Through a maze of bulging packing boxes and barrels she picked her way to a faded rose-colored chair that flanked the fire-place. That the chair was already half occupied by a pile of ancient books and four dusty garden trowels only served to intensify the general air of gloom. Presiding over all, two dreadful bouquets of long-dead grasses flared wanly on the mantle-piece. And from the tattered old landscape paper on the walls Civil War heroes stared regretfully down through pale and tarnished frames.

"Dear me ... dear me," shivered Flame. "They're not going to Christmas at all ... evidently! Not a sprig of holly anywhere! Not a ravel of tinsel! Not a jingle bell!... Oh she must have lost a lot of lovers," thrilled Flame. "I can bring her flowers, anyway! My very first Paper White Narcissus! My--."

With a scrape of the foot the Butler made known his return.

"Miss Flora!" he announced.

With a catch of her breath Flame jumped to her feet and turned to greet the biggest, ugliest, most brindled, most wizened Bull Dog she had ever seen in her life.

"*Miss Flora!*" repeated the old Butler succinctly.

"Miss Flora?" gasped Flame. "Why.... Why, I thought Miss Flora was a Lady! Why--"

"Miss Flora is indeed a very grand lady, Miss!" affirmed the Butler without a flicker of expression. "Of a pedigree so famous ... so distinguished ... so ..." Numerically on his fingers he began to count the distinctions. "Five prizes this year! And three last! Do you mind the chop?" he gloated. "The breadth! The depth!... Did you never hear of alauntes?" he demanded. "Them bull-baiting dogs that was invented by the second Duke of York or thereabouts in the year 1406?"

"Oh my Glory!" thrilled Flame. "Is Miss Flora as old as *that*?"

"Miss Flora," said the old Butler with some dignity, "is young--hardly two in fact--so young that she seems to me but just weaned."

With her great eyes goggled to a particularly disconcerting sort of scrutiny Miss Flora sprang suddenly forward to investigate the visitor.

As though by a preconcerted signal a chair crashed over in the hall and the wolf hound and the setter and the coach dog came hurtling back in a furiously cordial onslaught. With wags and growls and yelps of joy all four dogs met in Flame's lap.

"They seem to like me, don't they?" triumphed Flame. Intermittently through the melee of flapping ears,--shoving shoulders,--waving paws, her beaming little face proved the absolute sincerity of that triumph. "Mother's never let me have any dogs," she confided. "Mother thinks they're not--Oh, of course, I realize that four dogs is a--a good many," she hastened diplomatically to concede to a certain sudden droop around the old Butler's mouth corners.

From his slow, stooping poke of the sulky fire the old Butler glanced up with a certain plaintive intentness.

"All dogs is too many," he affirmed.

"Come Christmas time I wishes I was dead."

"Wish you were dead ... at Christmas Time?" cried Flame. Acute shock was in her protest.

"It's the feedin'," sighed the old Butler. "It ain't that I mind eatin' with them on All Saints' Day or Fourth of July or even Sundays. But come Christmas Time it seems like I craves to eat with More Humans.... I got a nephew less'n twenty miles away. He's got cider in his cellar. And plum puddings. His woman she raises guinea chickens. And mince pies there is. And tasty gravies.--But me I mixes dog bread and milk--dog bread and milk--till I can't see nothing--think nothing but mush. And him with cider in his cellar!... It ain't as though Mr. Delcote ever came himself to prove anything," he argued. "Not he! Not Christmas Time! It's travelling he is.... He's had ... misfortunes," he confided darkly. "He travels for 'em same as some folks travels for their healths. Most especially at Christmas Time he travels for his misfortunes! He ..."

"*Mr. Delcote*?" quickened Flame. "Mr. Delcote?" (Now at last was the mysterious tenancy about to be divulged?)

"All he says," persisted the old Butler. "All he says is 'Now Barret,'--that's me, 'Now Barret I trust your honor to see that the dogs ain't neglected just because it's Christmas. There ain't no reason, Barret', he says, 'why innocent dogs should suffer Christmas just because everybody else does. They ain't done nothing.... It won't do now Barret', he says, 'for you to give 'em their dinner at dawn when they ain't accustomed to it, and a pail of water, and shut 'em up while you go off for the day with any barrel of cider. You know what dogs is, Barret', he says. 'And what they isn't. They've got to be fed regular', he says, 'and with discipline. Else there's deaths.--Some natural. Some unnatural. And some just plain spectacular from furniture falling on their arguments. So if there's any fatalities come this Christmas Time, Barret', he says, 'or any undue gains in weight or losses in weight, I shall infer, Barret', he says, 'that you was absent without leave.' ... It don't look like a very wholesome Christmas for me," sighed the old Butler. "Not either way. Not what you'd call wholesome."

"But this Mr. Delcote?" puzzled Flame. "What a perfectly horrid man he must be to give such heavenly dogs nothing but dog-bread and milk for their Christmas dinner!... Is he young? Is he old? Is he thin? Is he fat? However in the world did he happen to come to a queer, battered old place like the Rattle-Pane House? But once come why didn't he stay? And--And--And--?"

"Yes'm," sighed the old Butler.

In a ferment of curiosity, Flame edged jerkily forward, and subsided as jerkily again.

"Oh, if this only was a Parish Call," she deprecated, "I could ask questions right out loud. 'How? Where? Why? When?' ... But being just a social call--I suppose--I suppose...?" Appealingly her eager eyes searched the old Butler's inscrutable face.

"Yes'm," repeated the old Butler dully. Through the quavering fingers that he swept suddenly across his brow two very genuine tears glistened.

With characteristic precipitousness Flame jumped to her feet.

"Oh, darn Mr. Delcote!" she cried. "I'll feed your dogs, Christmas Day! It won't take a minute after my own dinner or before! I'll run like the wind! No one need ever know!"

So it was that when Flame arrived at her own home fifteen minutes later, and found her parents madly engaged in packing suit-cases, searching time-tables, and rushing generally to and fro from attic to cellar, no very mutual exchange of confidences ensued.

"It's your Uncle Wally!" panted her Mother.

"Another shock!" confided her Father.

"Not such a bad one, either," explained her Mother. "But of course we'll have to go! The very first thing in the morning! Christmas Day, too! And leave you all alone! It's a perfect shame! But I've planned it all out for everybody! Father's Lay Reader, of course, will take the Christmas service! We'll just have to omit the Christmas Tree surprise for the children!... It's lucky we didn't even unpack the trimmings! Or tell a soul about it." In a hectic effort to pack both a thick coat and a thin coat and a thick dress and a thin dress and thick boots and thin boots in the same suit-case she began very palpably to pant again. "Yes! Every detail is all planned out!" she asserted with a breathy sort of pride. "You and your Father are both so flighty I don't know whatever in the world you'd do if I didn't plan out everything for you!"

With more manners than efficiency Flame and her Father dropped at once every helpful thing they were doing and sat down in rocking chairs to listen to the plan.

"Flame, of course, can't stay here all alone. Flame's Mother turned and confided *sotto voce* to her husband. Young men might call. The Lay Reader is almost sure to call.... He's a dear delightful soul of course, but I'm afraid he has an amorous eye."

"All Lay Readers have amorous eyes," reflected her husband. "Taken all in all it is a great asset."

"Don't be flippant!" admonished Flame's Mother. "There are reasons ... why I prefer that Flame's first offer of marriage should not be from a Lay Reader."

"Why?" brightened Flame.

"S--sh--," cautioned her Father.

"Very good reasons," repeated her Mother. From the conglomerate packing under her hand a puff of spilled tooth-powder whiffed fragrantly into the air.

"Yes?" prodded her husband's blandly impatient voice.

"Flame shall go to her Aunt Minna's" announced the dominant maternal voice. "By driving with us to the station, she'll have only two hours to wait for her train, and that will save one bus fare! Aunt Minna is a vegetarian and doesn't believe in sweets either, so that will be quite a unique and profitable experience for Flame to add to her general culinary education! It's a wonderful house!... A bit dark of course! But if the day should prove at all bright,--not so bright of course that Aunt Minna wouldn't be willing to have the shades up, but--Oh and Flame," she admonished still breathlessly, "I think you'd better be careful to wear one of your rather longish skirts! And oh do be sure to wipe your feet every time you come in! And don't chatter! Whatever you do, don't chatter! Your Aunt Minna, you know, is just a little bit peculiar! But such a worthy woman! So methodical! So...."

To Flame's inner vision appeared quite suddenly the pale, inscrutable face of the old Butler who asked nothing,--answered nothing,--welcomed nothing,--evaded nothing.

"... Yes'm," said Flame.

But it was a very frankly disconsolate little girl who stole late that night to her Father's study, and perched herself high on the arm of his chair with her cheek snuggled close to his.

"Of Father-Funny," whispered Flame, "I've got such a queer little pain."

"A pain?" jerked her Father. "Oh dear me! Where is it? Go and find your Mother at once!"

"Mother?" frowned Flame. "Oh it isn't that kind of a pain.--It's in my Christmas. I've got such a sad little pain in my Christmas."

"Oh dear me--dear me!" sighed her Father. Like two people most precipitously smitten with shyness they sat for a moment staring blankly around the room at every conceivable object except each other. Then quite suddenly they looked back at each other and smiled.

"Father," said Flame. "You're not of course a very old man.... But still you are pretty old, aren't you? You've seen a whole lot of Christmasses, I mean?"

"Yes," conceded her Father.

From the great clumsy rolling collar of her blanket wrapper Flame's little face loomed suddenly very pink and earnest.

"But Father," urged Flame. "Did you ever in your whole life spend a Christmas just exactly the way you wanted to? Honest-to-Santa Claus now,--did you *ever*?"

"Why--Why, no," admitted her Father after a second's hesitation. "Why no, I don't believe I ever did." Quite frankly between his brows there puckered a very black frown. "Now take to-morrow, for instance," he complained. "I had planned to go fishing through the ice.... After the morning service, of course,-- after we'd had our Christmas dinner,--and gotten tired of our presents,--every intention in the world I had of going fishing through the ice.... And now your Uncle Wally has to go and have a shock! I don't believe it was necessary. He should have taken extra precautions. The least that delicate relatives can do is to take extra precautions at holiday time.... Oh, of course your Uncle Wally has books in his library," he brightened, "very interesting old books that wouldn't be perfectly seemly for a minister of the Gospel to have in his own library.... But still it's very disappointing," he wilted again.

"I agree with you ... utterly, Father-Funny!" said Flame. "But ... Father," she persisted, "Of all the people you know in the world,--millions would it be?"

"No, call it thousands" corrected her Father.

"Well, thousands," accepted Flame. "Old people, young people, fat people, skinnys, cross people, jolly people?... Did you ever in your life know *any one* who had ever spent Christmas just the way he wanted to?"

"Why ... no, I don't know that I ever did," considered her Father. With his elbows on the arms of his chair, his slender fingers forked to a lovely Gothic arch above the bridge of his nose, he yielded himself instantly to the reflection. "Why ... no, ... I don't know that I ever did," he repeated with an increasing air of conviction.... "When you're young enough to enjoy the day as a 'holler' day there's usually some blighting person who prefers to have it observed as a holy day.... And by the time you reach an age where you really rather appreciate its being a holy day the chances are that you've got a houseful of racketty youngsters who fairly insist on reverting to the 'holler' day idea again."

"U--m--m," encouraged Flame.

--"When you're little, of course," mused her Father, "you have to spend the day the way your elders want you to!... You crave a Christmas Tree but they prefer stockings! You yearn to skate but they consider the weather better for corn-popping! You ask for a bicycle but they had already found a very nice bargain in flannels! You beg to dine the gay-kerchiefed Scissor-Grinder's child, but they invite the Minister's toothless mother-in-law!... And when you're old enough to go courting," he sighed, "your lady-love's sentiments are outraged if you don't spend the day with her and your own family are perfectly furious if you don't spend the day with them!... And after you're married?" With a gesture of ultimate despair he sank back into his cushions. "N--o, no one, I suppose, in the whole world, has ever spent Christmas just exactly the way he wanted to!"

"Well, I," triumphed Flame, "have got a chance to spend Christmas just exactly the way I want to!... The one chance perhaps in a life-time, it would seem!... No heart aches involved, no hurt feelings, no disappointments for anybody! Nobody left out! Nobody dragged in! Why Father-Funny," she cried. "It's an experience that might distinguish me all my life long! Even when I'm very old and crumpled people would point me out on the street and say *'There's* some one who once spent Christmas just exactly the way she wanted to'!!" To a limpness almost unbelievable the eager little figure wilted down within its blanket-wrapper swathings. "And now ..." deprecated Flame, "Mother has gone and wished me on Aunt Minna instead!" With a sudden revival of enthusiasm two small hands crept out of their big cuffs and clutched her Father by the ears.

**KARTINDO PUBLISHING HOUSE (Kartindo.com)**

"Oh Father-Funny!" pleaded Flame. "If you were too old to want it for a 'holler' day and not quite old enough to need it for a holy day ... so that all you asked in the world was just to have it a *holly* day! Something all bright! Red and green! And tinsel! and jingle-bells!... How would you like to have Aunt Minna wished on you?... It isn't you know as though Aunt Minna was a--a pleasant person," she argued with perfectly indisputable logic. "You couldn't wish one 'A Merry Aunt Minna' any more than you could wish 'em a 'Merry Good Friday'!" From the clutch on his ears the small hands crept to a point at the back of his neck where they encompassed him suddenly in a crunching hug. "Oh Father-Funny!" implored Flame, "You were a Lay Reader once! You must have had *very* amorous eyes! Couldn't you *please* persuade Mother that..."

With a crisp flutter of skirts Flame's Mother, herself, appeared abruptly in the door. Her manner was very excited.

"Why wherever in the world have you people been?" she cried. "Are you stone deaf? Didn't you hear the telephone? Couldn't you even hear me calling? Your Uncle Wally is worse! That is he's better but he thinks he's worse! And they want us to come at once! It's something about a new will! The Lawyer telephoned! He advises us to come at once! They've sent an automobile for us! It will be here any minute!... But whatever in the world shall we do about Flame?" she cried distractedly. "You know how Uncle Wally feels about having young people in the house! And she can't possibly go to Aunt Minna's till to-morrow! And...."

"But you see I'm not going to Aunt Minna's!" announced Flame quite serenely. Slipping down from her Father's lap she stood with a round, roly-poly flannel sort of dignity confronting both her parents. "Father says I don't have to!"

"Why, Flame!" protested her Father.

"No, of course, you didn't say it with your mouth," admitted Flame. "But you said it with your skin and bones!--I could feel it working."

"Not go to your Aunt Minna's?" gasped her Mother. "What do you want to do?... Stay at home and spend Christmas with the Lay Reader?"

"When you and Father talk like that," murmured Flame with some hauteur, "I don't know whether you're trying to run him down ... or run him up."

"Well, how do you feel about him yourself?" veered her Father quite irrelevantly.

**KARTINDO PUBLISHING HOUSE (Kartindo.com)**

"Oh, I like him--some," conceded Flame. In her bright cheeks suddenly an even brighter color glowed. "I like him when he leaves out the Litany," she said. "I've told him I like him when he leaves out the Litany.--He's leaving it out more and more I notice.--Yes, I like him very much."

"But this Aunt Minna business," veered back her Father suddenly. "What *do* you want to do? That's just the question. What *do* you want to do?"

"Yes, what do you want to do?" panted her Mother.

"I want to make a Christmas for myself!" said Flame. "Oh, of course, I know perfectly well," she agreed, "that I could go to a dozen places in the Parish and be cry-babied over for my presumable loneliness. And probably I *should* cry a little," she wavered, "towards the dessert--when the plum pudding came in and it wasn't like Mother's.--But if I made a Christmas of my own--" she rallied instantly. "Everything about it would be brand-new and unassociated! I tell you I *want* to make a Christmas of my own! It's the chance of a life-time! Even Father sees that it's the chance of a life-time!"

"Do you?" demanded his wife a bit pointedly.

"*Honk-honk!*" screamed the motor at the door.

"Oh, dear me, whatever in the world shall I do?" cried Flame's Mother. "I'm almost distracted! I'm--"

"When in Doubt do as the Doubters do," suggested Flame's Father quite genially. "Choose the most doubtful doubt on the docket and--Flame's got a pretty level head," he interrupted himself very characteristically.

"No young girl has a level heart," asserted Flame's Mother. "I'm so worried about the Lay Reader."

"Lay Reader?" murmured her Father. Already he had crossed the threshold into the hall and was rummaging through an over-loaded hat rack for his fur coat. "Why, yes," he called back, "I quite forgot to ask. Just what kind of a Christmas is it, Flame, that you want to make?" With unprecedented accuracy he turned at the moment to force his wife's arms into the sleeves of her own fur coat.

Twice Flame rolled up her cuffs and rolled them down again before she answered.

"I--I want to make a Surprise for Miss Flora," she confided.

"*Honk-honk!*" urged the automobile.

"For Miss Flora?" gasped her Mother.

"Miss Flora?" echoed her Father.

"Why, at the Rattle-Pane House, you know!" rallied Flame. "Don't you remember that I called there this afternoon? It--it looked rather lonely there.--I--think I could fix it."

"Honk-honk-honk!" implored the automobile.

"But who *is* this Miss Flora?" cried her Mother. "I never heard anything so ridiculous in my life! How do we know she's respectable?"

"Oh, my dear," deprecated Flame's Father. "Just as though the owners of the Rattle-Pane House would rent it to any one who wasn't respectable!"

"Oh, she's *very* respectable," insisted Flame. "Of a lineage so distinguished--"

"How old might this paragon be?" queried her Father.

"Old?" puzzled Flame. To her startled mind two answers only presented themselves.... Should she say "Oh, she's only just weaned," or "Well,--she was invented about 1406?" Between these two dilemmas a single compromise suggested itself. "She's *awfully* wrinkled," said Flame; "that is--her face is. All wizened up, I mean."

"Oh, then of course she *must* be respectable," twinkled Flame's Father.

"And is related in some way," persisted Flame, "to Edward the 2nd--Duke of York."

"Of that guarantee of respectability I am, of course, not quite so sure," said her Father.

With a temperish stamping of feet, an infuriate yank of the door-bell, Uncle Wally's chauffeur announced that the limit of his endurance had been reached.

Blankly Flame's Mother stared at Flame's Father. Blankly Flame's Father returned the stare.

"Oh, *p-l-e-a-s-e*!" implored Flame. Her face was crinkled like fine crêpe.

"Smooth out your nose!" ordered her Mother. On the verge of capitulation the same familiar fear assailed her. "Will you promise not to see the Lay Reader?" she bargained.

"--Yes'm," said Flame.

# *PART II*

It's a dull person who doesn't wake up Christmas Morning with a

curiously ticklish sense of Tinsel in the pit of his stomach!--A sort of a Shine!
A kind of a Pain!

"Glisten and Tears, Pang of the years."

That's Christmas!

So much was born on Christmas Day! So much has died! So much is yet to
come! Balsam-Scented, with the pulse of bells, how the senses sing! Memories
that wouldn't have batted an eye for all the Gabriel Trumpets in Eternity
leaping to life at the sound of a twopenny horn! Merry Folk who were with us
once and are no more! Dream Folk who have never been with us yet but will be
some time! Ache of old carols! Zest of new-fangled games! Flavor of
puddings! Shine of silver and glass! The pleasant frosty smell of the Express-
man! The Gift Beautiful! The Gift Dutiful! The Gift that Didn't Come! *Heigho*!
Manger and Toy-Shop,--Miracle and Mirth,--

"Glisten and Tears, LAUGH at the years!"

*That's* Christmas!

Flame Nourice certainly was willing to laugh at the years. Eighteen usually is!

Waking at Dawn two single thoughts consumed her,--the Lay Reader, and the
humpiest of the express packages downstairs.

The Lay Reader's name was Bertrand. "Bertrand the Lay Reader," Flame
always called him. The rest of the Parish called him Mr. Laurello.

It was the thought of Bertrand the Lay Reader that made Flame laugh the most.

"As long as I've promised most faithfully not to see him," she laughed, "how
can I possibly go to church? For the first Christmas in my life," she laughed, "I
won't have to go to church!"

With this obligation so cheerfully canceled, the exploration of the humpiest express package loomed definitely as the next task on the horizon.

Hoping for a fur coat from her Father, fearing for a set of encyclopedias from her Mother, she tore back the wrappings with eager hands only to find,--all-astonished, and half a-scream,--a gay, gauzy layer of animal masks nosing interrogatively up at her. Less practical surely than the fur coat,--more amusing, certainly, than encyclopedias,--the funny "false faces" grinned up at her with a curiously excitative audacity. Where from?--No identifying card! What for? No conceivable clew!--Unless perhaps just on general principles a donation for the Sunday School Christmas Tree?--But there wasn't going to be any tree! Tentatively she reached into the box and touched the fiercely striped face of a tiger, the fantastically exaggerated beak of a red and green parrot. "U-m-m-m," mused Flame. "Whatever in the world shall I do with them?" Then quite abruptly she sank back on her heels and began to laugh and laugh and laugh. Even the Lay Reader had not received such a laughing But even to herself she did not say just what she was laughing at. It was a time for deeds, it would seem, and not for words.

Certainly the morning was very full of deeds!

There was, of course, a present from her Mother to be opened,--warm, woolly stockings and things like that. But no one was ever swerved from an original purpose by trying on warm, woolly stockings. And from her Father there was the most absurd little box no bigger than your nose marked, "For a week in New York," and stuffed to the brim with the sweetest bright green dollar bills. But, of course, you couldn't try those on. And half the Parish sent presents. But no Parish ever sent presents that needed to be tried on. No gay, fluffy scarfs,--no lacey, frivolous pettiskirts,--no bright delaying hat-ribbons! Just books,--illustrated poems usually, very wholesome pickles,--and always a huge motto to recommend, "Peace on Earth, Good Will to Men."--To "Men"?--Why not to Women?--Why not at least to "*Dogs*?" questioned Flame quite abruptly.

Taken all in all it was not a Christmas Morning of sentiment but a Christmas morning of *works*! Kitchen works, mostly! Useful, flavorous adventures with a turkey! A somewhat nervous sally with an apple pie! Intermittently, of course, a few experiments with flour paste! A flaire or two with a paint brush! An errand to the attic! Interminable giggles!

Surely it was four o'clock before she was even ready to start for the Rattle-Pane House. And "starting" is by no means the same as arriving. Dragging a sledful of miscellaneous Christmas goods an eighth of a mile over bare ground is not an easy task. She had to make three tugging trips. And each start was delayed by her big gray pussy cat stealing out to try to follow her. And each arrival complicated by the yelpings and leapings and general cavortings of four dogs who didn't see any reason in the world why they shouldn't escape from their forced imprisonment in the shed-yard and prance home with her. Even with the third start and the third arrival finally accomplished, the crafty cat stood waiting for her on the steps of the Rattle-Pane House,--back arched, fur bristled, spitting like some new kind of weather-cock at the storm in the shed-yard, and had to be thrust quite unceremoniously into a much too small covered basket and lashed down with yards and yards of tinsel that was needed quite definitely for something else.--It isn't just the way of the Transgressor that's hard.--Nobody's way is any too easy!

The door-key, though, was exactly where the old Butler had said it would be,--under the door mat, and the key itself turned astonishingly cordially in the rusty old lock. Never in her whole little life having owned a door-key to her own house it seemed quite an adventure in itself to be walking thus possessively through an unfamiliar hall into an absolutely unknown kitchen and goodness knew what on either side and beyond.

Perfectly simply too as the old Butler had promised, the four dog dishes, heaping to the brim, loomed in prim line upon the kitchen table waiting for distribution.

"U-m-m," sniffed Flame. "Nothing but mush! *Mush*!--All over the world to-day I suppose--while their masters are feasting at other people's houses on puddings and--and cigarettes! How the poor darlings must suffer! Locked in sheds! Tied in yards! Stuffed down cellar!"

"Me-o-w," twinged a plaintive hint from the hallway just outside.

"Oh, but cats are different," argued Flame. "So soft, so plushy, so spineless! Cats were *meant* to be stuffed into things."

Without further parleying she doffed her red tam and sweater, donned a huge white all-enveloping pinafore, and started to ameliorate as best she could the Christmas sufferings of the "poor darlings" immediately at hand.

It was at least a yellow kitchen,--or had been once. In all that gray, dank, neglected house, the one suggestion of old sunshine.

"We shall have our dinner here," chuckled Flame. "After the carols--we shall have our dinner here."

Very boisterously in the yard just outside the window the four dogs scuffled and raced for sheer excitement and joy at this most unexpected advent of human companionship. Intermittently from time to time by the aid of old boxes or barrels they clawed their way up to the cobwebby window-sill to peer at the strange proceedings. Intermittently from time to time they fell back into the frozen yard in a chaos of fur and yelps.

By five o'clock certainly the faded yellow kitchen must have looked very strange, even to a dog!

Straight down its dingy, wobbly-floored center stretched a long table cheerfully spread with "the Rev. Mrs. Flamande Nourice's" second best table cloth. Quaint high-backed chairs dragged in from the shadowy parlor circled the table. A pleasant china plate gleamed like a hand-painted moon before each chair. At one end of the table loomed a big brown turkey; at the other, the appropriate vegetables. Pies, cakes, and doughnuts, interspersed themselves between. Green wreaths streaming with scarlet ribbons hung nonchalantly across every chair-top. Tinsel garlands shone on the walls. In the doorway reared a hastily constructed mimicry of a railroad crossing sign.

[Illustration]

Directly opposite and conspicuously placed above the rusty stove-pipe stretched the Parish's Gift Motto--duly re-adjusted.

"*Peace* on *Earth*, Good Will to *Dogs*."

"Fatuously silly," admitted Flame even to herself. "But yet it does add something to the Gayety of Rations!"

Stepping aside for a single thrilling moment to study the full effect of her handiwork, the first psychological puzzle of her life smote sharply across her senses. Namely, that you never really get the whole fun out of anything unless you are absolutely alone.--But the very first instant you find yourself absolutely alone with a Really-Good-Time you begin to twist and turn and hunt about for somebody Very Special to share it with you!

The only "Very Special" person that Flame could think of was "Bertrand the Lay Reader."

All a-blush with the sheer mental surprise of it she fled to the shed door to summon the dogs.

"Maybe even the dogs won't come!" she reasoned hectically. "Maybe nothing will come! Maybe that's always the way things happen when you get your own way about something else!"

Like a blast from the Arctic the Christmas twilight swept in on her. It crisped her cheeks,--crinkled her hair! Turned her spine to a wisp of tinsel! All outdoors seemed suddenly creaking with frost! All indoors, with *unknownness*!

"Come, Beautiful-Lovely!" she implored. "Come, Lopsy! Miss Flora! Come, Blunder-Blot!'"

But there was really no need of entreaty. A turn of the door-knob would have brought them! Leaping, loping, four abreast, they came plunging like so many North Winds to their party! Streak of Snow,--Glow of Fire,--Frozen Mud--Sun-Spot!--Yelping-mouthed--slapping-tailed! Backs bristling! Legs stiffening! Wolf Hound, Setter, Bull Dog, Dalmatian,--each according to his kind, hurtling, crowding!

"Oh, dear me, dear me," struggled Flame. "Maybe a carol would calm them."

To a certain extent a carol surely did. The hair-cloth parlor of the Rattle-Pane House would have calmed anything. And the mousey smell of the old piano fairly jerked the dogs to its senile old ivory keyboard. Cocking their ears to its quavering treble notes,--snorting their nostrils through its gritty guttural basses, they watched Flame's facile fingers sweep from sound to sound.

"Oh, what a--glorious lark!" quivered Flame. "What a--a *lonely* glorious lark!"

Timidly at first but with an increasing abandon, half laughter and half tears, the clear young soprano voice took up its playful paraphrase,

"God rest you merrie--animals! Let nothing you dismay!"

caroled Flame.

"For--"

It was just at this moment that Beautiful-Lovely, the Wolf Hound,--muzzled lifted, eyes rolling, jabbed his shrill nose into space and harmony with a carol of his own,--octaves of agony,--Heaven knows what of ecstasy,--that would have hurried an owl to its nest, a ghoul to a moving picture show!

"Wow-Wow--*Wow*!" caroled Beautiful-Lovely. "Ww--ow--Ww--ow--*Ww--Oo- -Wwwww*!"

As Flame's hands dropped from the piano the unmistakable creak of red wheels sounded on the frozen driveway just outside.

No one but "Bertrand the Lay Reader" drove a buggy with red wheels! To the infinite scandalization of the Parish--no one but "Bertrand the Lay Reader" drove a buggy with red wheels!--Fleet steps sounded suddenly on the path! Startled fists beat furiously on the door!

"What is it? What is it?" shouted a familiar voice. "Whatever in the world is happening? Is it *murder*? Let me in! *Let me in!*"

"Sil--ly!" hissed Flame through a crack in the door. "It's nothing but a party! Don't you know a--a party when you hear it?"

For an instant only, blank silence greeted her confidence. Then "Bertrand the Lay Reader" relaxed in an indisputably genuine gasp of astonishment.

"Why! Why, is that you, Miss Flame?" he gasped. "Why, I thought it was a murder! Why--Why, whatever in the world are you doing here?"

"I--I'm having a party," hissed Flame through the key-hole.

"A--a--party?" stammered the Lay Reader. "Open the door!"

"No, I--can't," said Flame.

"Why not?" demanded the Lay Reader.

Helplessly in the darkness of the vestibule Flame looked up,--and down,--and sideways,--but met always in every direction the memory of her promise.

"I--I just can't," she admitted a bit weakly. "It wouldn't be convenient.--I--I've got trouble with my eyes."

"Trouble with your eyes?" questioned the Lay Reader.

"I didn't go away with my Father and Mother," confided Flame.

"No,--so I notice," observed the Lay Reader. "*Please* open the door!"

"Why?" parried Flame.

"I've been looking for you everywhere," urged the Lay Reader. "At the Senior Warden's! At all the Vestrymen's houses! Even at the Sexton's! I knew you didn't go away! The Garage Man told me there were only two!--I thought surely I'd find you at your own house.--But I only found sled tracks."

"That was me,--I," mumbled Flame.

"And then I heard these awful screams," shuddered the Lay Reader.

"That was a Carol," said Flame.

"A Carol?" scoffed the Lay Reader. "Open the door!"

"Well--just a crack," conceded Flame.

It was astonishing how a man as broad-shouldered as the Lay Reader could pass so easily through a crack.

Conscience-stricken Flame fled before him with her elbow crooked across her forehead.

"Oh, my eyes! My eyes!" she cried.

"Well, really," puzzled the Lay Reader. "Though I claim, of course, to be ordinarily bright--I had never suspected myself of being actually dazzling."

"Oh, you're not bright at all," protested Flame. "It's just my promise.--I promised Mother not to see you!"

"Not to see *me*?" questioned the Lay Reader. It was astonishing how almost instantaneously a man as purely theoretical as the Lay Reader was supposed to be, thought of a perfectly practical solution to the difficulty. "Why--why we might tie my big handkerchief across your eyes," he suggested. "Just till we get this mystery straightened out.--Surely there is nothing more or less than just plain righteousness in--that!"

**KARTINDO PUBLISING HOUSE (Kartindo.com)**

"What a splendid idea!" capitulated Flame. "But, of course, if I'm absolutely blindfolded," she wavered for a second only, "you'll have to lead me by the hand."

"I could do that," admitted the Lay Reader.

With the big white handkerchief once tied firmly across her eyes, Flame's last scruple vanished.

"Well, you see," she began quite precipitously, "I *did* think it would be such fun to have a party!--A party all my own, I mean!--A party just exactly as I wanted it! No Parish in it at all! Or good works! Or anything! Just *fun*!--And as long as Mother and Father had to go away anyway--" Even though the blinding bandage the young eyes seemed to lift in a half wistful sort of appeal. "You see there's some sort of property involved," she confided quite impulsively. "Uncle Wally's making a new will. There's a corn-barn and a private chapel and a collection of Chinese lanterns and a piebald pony principally under dispute.-- Mother, of course thinks we ought to have the corn-barn. But Father can't decide between the Chinese lanterns and the private chapel.--Personally," she sighed, "I'm hoping for the piebald pony."

"Yes, but this--party?" prodded the Lay Reader.

"Oh, yes,--the party--" quickened Flame.

"Why have it in a deserted house?" questioned the Lay Reader with some incisiveness.

Even with her eyes closely bandaged Flame could see perfectly clearly that the Lay Reader was really quite troubled.

"Oh, but you see it isn't exactly a deserted house," she explained.

"Who lives here?" demanded the Lay Reader.

"I don't know--exactly," admitted Flame. "But the Butler is a friend of mine and--"

"The--Butler is a friend of yours?" gasped the Lay Reader. Already, if Flame could only have seen it, his head was cocked with sudden intentness towards the parlor door. "There is certainly something very strange about all this," he whispered a bit hectically. "I could almost have sworn that I heard a faint scuffle,--the horrid sound of a person--strangling."

"Strangling?" giggled Flame. "Oh, that is just the sound of Miss Flora's 'girlish glee'! If she'd only be content to chew the corner of the piano cover! But when she insists on inhaling it, too!"

"Miss Flora?" gasped the Lay Reader. "Is this a Mad House?"

"Miss Flora is a--a dog," confided Flame a bit coolly. "I neglected--it seems--to state that this is a dog-party that I'm having."

"*Dogs*?" winced the Lay Reader. "Will they bite?"

"Only if you don't trust them," confided Flame.

"But it's so hard to trust a dog that will bite you if you don't trust him," frowned the Lay Reader. "It makes such a sort of a--a vicious circle, as it were."

"Vicious Circe?" mused Flame, a bit absent-mindedly. "No, I don't think it's nice at all to call Miss Flora a 'Vicious Circe.'" It was Flame's turn now to wince back a little. "I--I hate people who hate dogs!" she cried out quite abruptly.

"Oh, I don't hate them," lied the Lay Reader like a gentleman, "it's only that-- that--. You see a dog bit me once!" he confided with significant emphasis.

"I--bit a dentist--once," mused Flame without any emphasis at all.

"Oh, but I say, Miss Flame," deprecated the Lay Reader. "That's different! When a dog bites you, you know, there's always more or less question whether he was mad or not."

"There doesn't seem to have been any question at all," mused Flame, "that *you* were mad! Did you have *your* head sent off to be investigated or anything?"

"Oh, I say, Miss Flame," implored the Lay Reader, "I tell you I *like* dogs,--good dogs! I assure you I'm very--oh, very much interested in this dog party of yours! Such a quaint idea! So--so--! If I could be of any possible assistance?" he implored.

"Maybe you could be," relaxed Flame ever so faintly. "But if you're really coming to my party," she stiffened again, "you've got to behave like my party!"

"Why, of course I'll behave like your party!" laughed the Lay Reader.

"There *is* a problem," admitted Flame. "Five problems, to be perfectly accurate.--Four dogs, and a cat in the wood-shed."

"And a cat in the wood-shed?" echoed the Lay Reader quite idiotically.

"The table is set," affirmed Flame. "The places, all ready!--But I don't know how to get the dogs into their chairs!--They run around so! They yelp! They jump!--They haven't had a mouthful to eat, you see, since last night, this time!--And when they once see the turkey I'm--I'm afraid they'll stampede it."

"Turkey?" quizzed the Lay Reader who had dined that day on corned beef.

"Oh, of course, mush was what they were intended to have," admitted Flame. "Piles and piles of mush! Extra piles and piles of mush I should judge because it was Christmas Day!... But don't you think mush does seem a bit dull?" she questioned appealingly. "For Christmas Day? Oh, I did think a turkey would taste so good!"

"It certainly would," conceded the Lay Reader.

"So if you'd help me--" wheedled Flame, "it would be well-worth staying blindfolded for.... For, of course, I shall have to stay blindfolded. But I can see a little of the floor," she admitted, "though I couldn't of course break my promise to my Mother by seeing you."

"No, certainly not," admitted the Lay Reader.

"Otherwise--" murmured Flame with a faint gesture towards the door.

"I will help you," said the Lay Reader.

"Where is your hand?" fumbled Flame.

"*Here*!" attested the Lay Reader.

"Lead us to the dogs!" commanded Flame.

Now the Captain of a ship feels genuinely obligated, it would seem, to go down with his ship if tragic circumstances so insist. But he never,--so far as I've ever heard, felt the slightest obligation whatsoever to go down with another captain's ship,--to be martyred in short for any job not distinctly his own. So Bertrand Lorello,--who for the cause he served, wouldn't have hesitated an instant probably, to be torn by Hindoo lions,--devoured by South Sea cannibals,--fallen upon by a chapel spire,--trampled to death even at a church rummage sale,--saw no conceivable reason at the moment for being eaten by dogs at a purely social function.

Even groping through a balsam-scented darkness with one hand clasping the thrilly fingers of a lovely young girl, this distaste did not altogether leave him.

"This--this mush that you speak of?" he questioned quite abruptly. "With the dogs as--as nervous as you say,--so unfortunately liable to stampede? Don't you think that perhaps a little mush served first,--a good deal of mush I would say, served first,--might act as a--as a sort of anesthetic?... Somewhere in the past I am almost sure I have read that mush in sufficient quantities, you understand, is really quite a--quite an anesthetic."

Very palpably in the darkness he heard a single throaty swallow.

"Lead us to the--mush," said Flame.

In another instant the door-knob turned in his hand, and the cheerful kitchen lamp-light,--glitter of tinsel,--flare of red ribbons,--savor of foods, smote sharply on him.

"Oh, I say, how *jolly*!" cried the Lay Reader.

"Don't let me bump into anything!" begged the blindfolded Flame, still holding tight to his hand.

"Oh, I say, Miss Flame," kindled the entranced Lay Reader, "it's *you* that look the jolliest! All in white that way! I've never seen you wear *that* to church, have I?"

"This is a pinafore," confided Flame coolly. "A bungalow apron, the fashion papers call it.... No, you've never seen me wear--this to church."

"O--h," said the Lay Reader.

"Get the mush," said Flame.

"The what?" asked the Lay Reader.

"It's there on the table by the window," gestured Flame. "Please set all four dishes on the floor,--each dish, of course, in a separate corner," ordered Flame. "There is a reason.... And then open the parlor door."

"Open the parlor door?" questioned the Lay Reader. It was no mere grammatical form of speech but a real query in the Lay Reader's mind.

"Well, maybe I'd better," conceded Flame. "Lead me to it."

Roused into frenzy by the sound of a stranger's step, a stranger's voice, the four dogs fumed and seethed on the other side of the panel.

"Sniff--Sniff--*Snort*!" the Red Setter sucked at the crack in the door.

"Woof! Woof! *Woof*!" roared the big Wolf Hound.

"Slam! Bang! Slash!" slapped the Dalmatian's crisp weight.

"Yi! Yi! Yi!" sang the Bull Dog.

"Hush! *Hush*, Dogs!" implored Flame. "This is Father's Lay Reader!"

"Your--Lay Reader!" contradicted the young man gallantly. It *was* pretty gallant of him, wasn't it? Considering everything?

In another instant four *shapes* with teeth in them came hurtling through!

If Flame had never in her life admired the Lay Reader she certainly would have admired him now for the sheer cold-blooded foresight which had presaged the inevitable reaction of the dogs upon the mush and the mush upon the dogs. With a single sniff at his heels, a prod of paws in his stomach, the onslaught swerved--and passed. Guzzlingly from four separate corners of the room issued sounds of joy and fulfillment.

With an impulse quite surprising even to herself Flame thrust both hands into the Lay Reader's clasp.

"You *are* nice, aren't you?" she quickened. In an instant of weakness one hand crept up to the blinding bandage, and recovered its honor as instantly. "Oh, I do wish I *could* see you," sighed Flame. "You're so good-looking! Even Mother thinks you're *so* good-looking!... Though she does get awfully worked up, of course, about your 'amorous eyes'!"

"Does your Mother think I've got ... 'amorous eyes'?" asked the Lay Reader a bit tersely. Behind his spectacles as he spoke the orbs in question softened and glowed like some rare exotic bloom under glass. "Does your Mother ... think I've got amorous eyes?"

"Oh, yes!" said Flame.

"And your Father?" drawled the Lay Reader.

"Why, Father says *of course* you've got 'amorous eyes'!" confided Flame with the faintest possible tinge of surprise at even being asked such a question. "That's the funny thing about Mother and Father," chuckled Flame. "They're always saying the same thing and meaning something entirely different by it. Why, when Mother says with her mouth all pursed up, 'I have every reason to believe that Mr. Lorello is engaged to the daughter of the Rector in his former Parish,' Father just puts back his head and howls, and says, 'Why, *of course*, Mr. Lorello is engaged to the daughter of the Rector in his former Parish! All Lay Readers....'"

In the sudden hush that ensued a faint sense of uneasiness flickered through Flame's shoulders.

"Is it you that have hushed? Or the dogs?" she asked.

"The dogs," said the Lay Reader.

Very cautiously, absolutely honorably, Flame turned her back to the Lay Reader, and lifted the bandage just far enough to prove the Lay Reader's assertion.

Bulging with mush the four dogs lay at rest on rounding sides with limp legs straggling, or crouched like lions' heads on paws, with limpid eyes blinking above yawny mouths.

"O--h," crooned Flame. "How sweet! Only, of course, with what's to follow," she regretted thriftily, "it's an awful waste of mush.... Excelsior warmed in the oven would have served just as well."

At the threat of a shadow across her eyeball she jerked the bandage back into place.

"Now, Mr. Lorello," she suggested blithely, "if you'll get the Bibles...."

"Bibles?" stiffened the Lay Reader. "Bibles? Why, really, Miss Flame, I couldn't countenance any sort of mock service! Even just for--for quaintness,-- even for Christmas quaintness!"

"Mock service?" puzzled Flame. "Bibles?... Oh, I don't want you to preach out of 'em," she hastened perfectly amiably to explain. "All I want them for is to plump-up the chairs.... The seats you see are too low for the dogs.... Oh, I suppose dictionaries would do," she compromised reluctantly. "Only dictionaries are always so scarce."

Obediently the Lay Reader raked the parlor book-cases for "plump-upable" books. With real dexterity he built Chemistries on Sermons and Ancient Poems on Cook Books till the desired heights were reached.

For a single minute more Flame took another peep at the table.

"Set a chair for yourself directly opposite me!" she ordered. For sheer hilarious satisfaction her feet began to dance and her hands to clap. "And whenever I really feel obliged to look," she sparkled, "you'll just have to leave the table, that's all!... And now...?" Appraisingly her muffled eye swept the shining vista. "Perfect!" she triumphed. "Perfect!" Then quite abruptly the eager mouth wilted. "Why ... Why I've forgotten the carving knife and fork!" she cried out in real distress. "Oh, how stupid of me!" Arduously, but without avail, she searched through all the drawers and cupboards of the Rattle-Pane kitchen. A single alternative occurred to her. "You'll have to go over to my house and get them,--Mr. Lorello!" she said. "Were you ever in my kitchen? Or my pantry?"

"No," admitted the Lay Reader.

"Well, you'll have to climb in through the window--someway," worried Flame. "I've mislaid my key somewhere here among all these dishes and boxes. And the pantry," she explained very explicitly, "is the third door on the right as you enter.... You'll see a chest of drawers. Open the second of 'em.... Or maybe you'd better look through all of them.... Only please ... please hurry!" Imploringly the little head lifted.

"If I hurry enough," said the Lay Reader quite impulsively, "may I have a kiss when I get back?"

"A kiss?" hooted Flame. In the curve of her cheek a dimple opened suddenly. "Well ... maybe," said Flame.

As though the word were wings the Lay Reader snatched his hat and sped out into the night.

It was astonishing how all the warm housey air seemed to rush out with him, and all the shivery frost rush back.

A little bit listlessly Flame dragged down the bandage from her eyes.

"It must be the creaks on the stairs that make it so awfully lonely all of a sudden," argued Flame. "It must be because the dogs snore so.... No mere man could make it so empty." With a precipitous nudge of the memory she dashed to the door and helloed to the fast retreating figure. "Oh, Bertrand! Bertrand!" she called, "I got sort of mixed up. It's the second door on the left! And if you don't find 'em there you'd better go up in Mother's room and turn out the silver chest! *Hurry!*"

Rallying back to the bright Christmas kitchen for the real business at hand, an accusing blush rose to the young spot where the dimple had been.

"Oh, Shucks!" parried Flame. "I kissed a Bishop before I was five!--What's a Lay Reader?" As one humanely willing to condone the future as well as the past she rolled up her white sleeves without further introspection, and dragged out from the protecting shadow of the sink the "humpiest box" which had so excited her emotions at home in an earlier hour of the day. Cracklingly under her eager fingers the clumsy cover slid off, exposing once more to her enraptured gaze the gay-colored muslin layer of animal masks leering fatuously up at her.

Only with her hand across her mouth did she keep from crying out. Very swiftly her glance traveled from the grinning muslin faces before her to the solemn fur faces on the other side of the room. The hand across her mouth tightened.

"Why, it's something like Creation," she giggled. "This having to decide which face to give to which animal!"

As expeditiously as possible she made her selection.

"Poor Miss Flora must be so tired of being so plain," she thought. "I'll give her the first choice of everything! Something really lovely! It can't help resting her!"

With this kind idea in mind she selected for Miss Flora a canary's face.--Softly yellow! Bland as treacle! Its swelling, tender muslin throat fairly reeking with the suggestion of innocent song! No one gazing once upon such ornithological purity would ever speak a harsh word again, even to a sparrow!

Nudging Miss Flora cautiously from her sonorous nap, Flame beguiled her with half a doughnut to her appointed chair, boosted her still cautiously to her pinnacle of books, and with various swift adjustments of fasteners, knotting of tie-strings,--an extra breathing hole jabbed through the beak, slipped the canary's beautiful blond countenance over Miss Flora's frankly grizzled mug.

For a single terrifying instant Miss Flora's crinkled sides tightened,--a snarl like ripped silk slipped through her straining lungs. Then once convinced that the mask was not a gas-box she accepted the liberty with reasonable *sang-froid* and sat blinking beadily out through the canary's yellow-rimmed eye-sockets with frank curiosity towards such proceedings as were about to follow. It was easy to see she was accustomed to sitting in chairs.

For the Wolf Hound Flame chose a Giraffe's head. Certain anatomical similarities seemed to make the choice wise. With a long vividly striped stockinet neck wrinkling like a mousquetaire glove, the neat small head that so closely fitted his own neat small head, the tweaked, interrogative ears,-- Beautiful-Lovely, the Wolf Hound, reared up majestically in his own chair. He also, once convinced that the mask was not a gas-box, resigned himself to the inevitable, and corporeally independent of such vain props as Chemistries or Sermons, lolled his fine height against the mahogany chair-back.

To Blunder-Blot, the trim Dalmatian, Flame assigned the Parrot's head, arrogantly beaked, gorgeously variegated, altogether querulous.

For Lopsy, the crafty Setter, she selected a White Rabbit's artless, pink-eared visage.

Yet out of the whole box of masks it had been the Bengal Tiger's fiercely bewhiskered visage that had fascinated Flame the most. Regretfully from its more or less nondescript companions, she picked up the Bengal Tiger now and pulled at its real, bristle-whiskers. In one of the chairs a dog stirred quite irrelevantly. Cocking her own head towards the wood-shed Flame could not be perfectly sure whether she heard a twinge of cat or a twinge of conscience. The unflinching glare of the Bengal Tiger only served to increase her self-reproach.

"After all," reasoned Flame, "it would be easy enough to set another place! And pile a few extra books!... I'm almost sure I saw a black plush bag in the parlor.... If the cat could be put in something like a black plush bag,--something perfectly enveloping like that? So that not a single line of its--its figure could be observed?... And it had a new head given it? A perfectly sufficient head-- like a Bengal Tiger?--I see no reason why--"

In five minutes the deed was accomplished. Its lovely sinuous "figure" reduced to the stolid contour of a black plush work-bag, its small uneasy head thrust into the roomy muslin cranium of the Bengal Tiger, the astonished Cat found herself slumping soggily on a great teetering pile of books, staring down as best she might through the Bengal Tiger's ear at the weirdest assemblage of animals which any domestic cat of her acquaintance had ever been forced to contemplate.

Coincidental with the appearance of the Cat a faint thrill passed through the rest of the company.... Nothing very much! No more, no less indeed, than passes through any company at the introduction of purely extraneous matter. From the empty plate which she had commandeered as a temporary pillow the Yellow Canary lifted an interrogative beak.... That was all! At Flame's left, the White-Haired Rabbit emitted an incongruous bark.... Scarcely worth reporting! Across the table the Giraffe thumped a white, plumy tail. Thoughtfully the Parrot's hooked nose slanted slightly to one side.

"Oh, I wish Bertrand would come!" fretted Flame. "Maybe this time he'll notice my 'Christmas Crossing' sign!" she chuckled with sudden triumph. "Talk about surprises!" Very diplomatically as she spoke she broke another doughnut in two and drew all the dogs' attention to herself. Almost hysterical with amusement she surveyed the scene before her. "Well, at least we can have 'grace' before the Preacher comes!" she laughed. A step on the gravel walk startled her suddenly. In a flash she had jerked down the blind-folding handkerchief across her eyes again, and folding her hands and the doughnut before her burst softly into paraphrase.

'Now we--sit us down to eat Thrice our share of Flesh and Sweet. If we should burst before we're through, Oh what in--Dogdom shall we do?'

**KARTINDO PUBLISING HOUSE (Kartindo.com)**

Thus it was that the Master of the House, returning unexpectedly to his unfamiliar domicile, stumbled upon a scene that might have shaken the reason of a less sober young man.

Startled first by the unwonted illumination from his kitchen windows, and second by the unprecedented aroma of Fir Balsam that greeted him even through the key-hole of his new front door, his feelings may well be imagined when groping through the dingy hall he first beheld the gallows-like structure reared in the kitchen doorway.

"My God!" he ejaculated, "Barrett is getting ready to hang himself! Gone mad probably--or something!"

Curdled with horror he forced himself to the object, only to note with convulsive relief but increasing bewilderment the cheerful phrasing and ultimate intent of the structure itself. "'Christmas Crossing'?" he repeated blankly. "'Look out for Surprises'?--'Shop, Cook, and Glisten'?" With his hand across his eyes he reeled back slightly against the wall. "It is I that have gone mad!" he gasped.

A little uncertain whether he was afraid of What-He-Was-About-to-See, or whether What-He-Was-About-to-See ought to be afraid of him, he craned his neck as best he could round the corner of the huge buffet that blocked the kitchen vista. A fresh bewilderment met his eyes. Where he had once seen cobwebs flapping grayly across the chimney-breast loomed now the gay worsted recommendation that *dogs specially*, should be considered in the Christmas Season. Throwing all caution aside he passed the buffet and plunged into the kitchen.

"Oh, *do* hurry!" cried an eager young voice. "I thought my hair would be white before you came!"

Like a man paralyzed he stopped short in his tracks to stare at the scene before him! The long, bright table! The absolutely formal food! A blindfolded girl! A perfectly strange blindfolded girl ... with her dark hair forty years this side of white--*begging him to hurry*!... A Black Velvet Bag surmounted by a Tiger's head stirring strangely in a chair piled high with books!... Seated next to the Black Velvet Bag a Canary as big as a Turkey Gobbler!... A Giraffe stepping suddenly forward with--with dog-paws thrust into his soup plate!... A White Rabbit heavily wreathed in holly rousing cautiously from his cushions!... A Parrot with a twitching black and white short-haired tail!... An empty chair facing the Girl! *An empty chair facing the Girl.*

"If this is *madness*," thought Delcote quite precipitously, "I am at least the Master of the Asylum!"

In another instant, with a prodigious stride he had slipped into the vacant seat.

"... So sorry to have kept you waiting," he murmured.

At the first sound of that unfamiliar voice, Flame yanked the handkerchief from her eyes, took one blank glance at the Stranger, and burst forth into a muffled, but altogether blood-curdling scream.

"Oh ... Oh ... Owwwwwwww!" said the scream.

As though waiting only for that one signal to break the spell of their enchantment, the Canary leaped upward and grabbed the Bengal Tiger by his muslin nose,--the White Rabbit sprang to "point" on the cooling turkey, and the Red and Green Parrot fell to the floor in a desperate effort to settle once and for all with the black spot that itched so impulsively on his left shoulder!

For a moment only, in comparative quiet, the Concerned struggled with the Concerned. Then true to all Dog Psychology,--absolutely indisputable, absolutely unalterable, the Non-Concerned leaped in upon the Non-Concerned! Half on his guard, but wholly on his itch, the jostled Parrot shot like a catapult across the floor! Lost to all sense of honor or table-manners the benign-faced Giraffe with his benign face still towering blandly in the air, burst through his own neck with a most curious anatomical effect,--locked his teeth in the Parrot's gay throat and rolled with him under the table in mortal combat!

Round and round the room spun the Yellow Canary and the Black Plush Bag!

Retreating as best she could from her muslin nose,--the Bengal Tiger or rather that which was within the Bengal Tiger, waged her war for Freedom! Ripping like a chicken through its shell she succeeded at last in hatching one front paw and one hind paw into action. Wallowing,--stumbling,--rolling,--yowling,--she humped from mantle-piece to chair-top, and from box to table.

Loyally the rabbit-eared Setter took up the chase. Mauled in the scuffle he ran with his meek face upside down! Lost to all reason, defiant of all morale, he proceeded to flush the game!

Dish-pans clattered, stools tipped over, pictures banged on the walls!

From her terrorized perch on the back of her chair Flame watched the fracas with dilated eyes.

Hunched in the hug of his own arms the Stranger sat rocking himself to and fro in uncontrollable, choking mirth,--"ribald mirth" was what Flame called it.

"Stop!" she begged. "Stop it! Somebody *stop* it!"

It was not until the Black Plush Bag at bay had ripped a red streak down Miss Flora's avid nose that the Stranger rose to interfere.

Very definitely then, with quick deeds, incisive words, he separated the immediate combatants, and ordered the other dogs into submission.

"Here you, Demon Direful!" he addressed the white Wolf Hound. "Drop that, Orion!" he shouted to the Irish Setter. "Cut it out, John!" he thundered at the Coach Dog.

"Their names are 'Beautiful-Lovely'!" cried Flame. "And 'Lopsy!' and 'Blunder-Blot!'"

With his hand on the Wolf Hound's collar, the Stranger stopped and stared up with frank astonishment, not to say resentment, at the girl's interference.

"Their names are *what*?" he said.

Something in the special intonation of the question infuriated Flame.... Maybe she thought his mouth scornful,--his narrowing eyes...? Goodness knows what she thought of his suddenly narrowing eyes!

In an instant she had jumped from her retreat to the floor.

"Who are you, anyway?" she demanded. "How dare you come here like this? Butting into my party!... And--and spoiling my discipline with the dogs! Who are you, I say?"

With Demon Direful, alias Beautiful-Lovely tugging wildly at his restraint, the Stranger's scornful mouth turned precipitously up, instead of down.

"Who am I?" he said. "Why, no one special at all except just--the Master of the House!"

**KARTINDO PUBLISING HOUSE (Kartindo.com)**

"*What*?" gasped Flame.

"Earle Delcote," bowed the Stranger.

With a little hand that trembled perfectly palpably Flame reached back to the arm of the big carved chair for support.

"Why--why, but Mr. Delcote is an old man," she gasped. "I'm almost sure he's an old man."

The smile on Delcote's mouth spread suddenly to his eyes.

"Not yet,--Thank God!" he bowed.

With a panic-stricken glance at doors, windows, cracks, the chimney pipe itself, Flame sank limply down in her seat again and gestured towards the empty place opposite her.

"Have a--have a chair," she stammered. Great tears welled suddenly to her eyes. "Oh, I--I know I oughtn't to be here," she struggled. "It's perfectly ... awful! I haven't the slightest right! Not the slightest! It's the--the cheekiest thing that any girl in the world ever did!... But your Butler said...! And he did so want to go away and--And I did so love your dogs! And I did so want to make *one* Christmas in the world just--exactly the way I wanted it! And--and--Mother and Father will be crazy!... And--and--"

Without a single glance at anything except herself, the Master of the House slipped back into his chair.

"Have a heart!" he said.

Flame did *not* accept this suggestion. With a very severe frown and downcast eyes she sat staring at the table. It seemed a very cheerless table suddenly, with all the dogs in various stages of disheveled finery grouped blatantly around their Master's chair.

"I can at least have my cat," she thought, "my--faithful cat!" In another instant she had slipped from the table, extracted poor Puss from a clutter of pans in the back of a cupboard, stripped the last shred of masquerade from her outraged form, and brought her back growling and bristling to perch on one arm of the high-backed chair. "Th--ere!" said Flame.

Glancing up from this innocent triumph, she encountered the eyes of the Master of the House fixed speculatively on the big turkey.

"I'm afraid everything is very cold," she confided with distinctly formal regret.

"Not for anything," laughed Delcote quite suddenly, "would I have kept you waiting--if I had only known."

Two spots of color glowed hotly in the girl's cheeks.

"It was not for you I was waiting," she said coldly.

"N--o?" teased Delcote. "You astonish me. For whom, then? Some incredible wight who, worse than late--isn't going to show up at all?... Heaven sent, I consider myself.... How else could so little a girl have managed so big a turkey?"

"There ... isn't any ... carving knife," whispered Flame.

The tears were glistening on her cheeks now instead of just in her eyes. A less observing man than Delcote might have thought the tears were really for the carving knife.

"What? No carving knife?" he roared imperiously. "And the house guaranteed 'furnished'?" Very furiously he began to hunt all around the kitchen in the most impossible places.

"Oh, it's furnished all right," quivered Flame. "It's just chock-full of dead things! Pressed flowers! And old plush bags! And pressed flowers! And--and pressed flowers!"

"Great Heavens!" groaned Delcote. "And I came here to forget 'dead things'!"

"Your--your Butler said you'd had misfortunes," murmured Flame.

"Misfortunes?" rallied Delcote. "I should think I had! In a single year I've lost health,--money,--most everything I own in the world except my man and my dogs!"

"They're ... good dogs," testified Flame.

"And the Doctor's sent me here for six months," persisted Delcote, "before he'll even hear of my plunging into things again!"

"Six months is a--a good long time," said Flame. "If you'd turn the hems we could make yellow curtains for the parlor in no time at all!"

"W--we?" stammered Delcote.

"M--Mother," said Flame. "... It's a long time since any dogs lived in the Rattle-Pane House."

"Rattle-*Brain* house?" bridled Delcote.

"Rattle-*Pane* House," corrected Flame.

A little bit worriedly Delcote returned to his seat.

"I shall have to rend the turkey, instead of carve it," he said.

"Rend it," acquiesced Flame.

In the midst of the rending a dark frown appeared between Delcote's eyes.

"These--these guests that you were expecting--?" he questioned.

"Oh, *stop*!" cried Flame. "Dreadful as I am I never--never would have dreamed of inviting 'guests'!"

"This 'guest' then," frowned Delcote. "Was he...?"

"Oh, you mean ... Bertrand?" flushed Flame. "Oh, truly, I didn't invite him! He just butted in ... same as you!"

"Same as ... I?" stammered Delcote.

"Well..." floundered Flame. "Well ... you know what I mean and ..."

With peculiar intentness the Master of the House fixed his eyes on the knotted white handkerchief which Flame had thrown across the corner of her chair.

"And is this 'Bertrand' person so ... so dazzling," he questioned, "that human eye may not look safely upon his countenance?"

"Bertrand ... dazzling?" protested Flame. "Oh, no! He's really quite dull.... It was only," she explained with sudden friendliness, "It was only that I had promised Mother not to 'see' him.... So, of course, when he butted in I...."

"O--h," relaxed the Master of the House. With a precipitous flippancy of manners which did not conform at all to the somewhat tragic austerity of his face he snatched up his knife and fork and thumped joyously on the table with the handles of them. "And some people talk about a country village being dull in the Winter Time!" he chuckled. "With a Dog's Masquerade and a Robbery at the Rectory all happening the same evening!" Grabbing her cat in her arms, Flame jerked her chair back from the table.

"A--a robbery at the Rectory?" she gasped. "Why--why, I'm the Rectory! I must go home at once!"

"Oh, Shucks!" shrugged the Master of the House. "It's all over now. But the people at the railroad station were certainly buzzing about it as I came through."

"B--buzzing about it?" articulated Flame with some difficulty.

Expeditiously the Master of the House resumed his rending of the turkey.

"Are you really from the Rectory?" he questioned. "How amusing.... Well, there's nothing really you could do about it now.... The constable and his prisoner are already on their way to the County Seat--wherever that may be. And a freshly 'burgled' house is rather a creepy place for a young girl to return to all alone.... Your parents are away, I believe?"

"Con--stable ... constable," babbled Flame quite idiotically.

"Yes, the regular constable was off Christmasing somewhere it seems, so he put a substitute on his job, a stranger from somewhere. Some substitute that! No mulling over hot toddies on Christmas night for him! He *saw* the marauder crawling in through the Rectory window! He *saw* him fumbling now to the left, now to the right, all through the front hall! He followed him up the stairs to a closet where the silver was evidently kept! He caught the man red-handed as it were! Or rather--white-handed," flushed the Master of the House for some quite unaccountable reason. "To be perfectly accurate," he explained conscientiously, "he was caught with a pair of--of--" Delicately he spelt out the word. "With a pair of--c-o-r-s-e-t-s rolled up in his hand. But inside the roll it seemed there was a solid silver--very elaborate carving set which the Parish had recently presented. The wretch was just unrolling it,--them, when he was caught."

"That was Bertrand!" said Flame. "My Father's Lay Reader."

It was the man's turn now to jump to his feet.

"*What*?" he cried.

"I sent him for the carving knife," said Flame.

"*What*?" repeated the man. Consternation versus Hilarity went racing suddenly like a cat-and-dog combat across his eyes.

"Yes," said Flame.

From the outside door the sound of furious knocking occurred suddenly.

"That sounds to me like--like parents' knocking," shivered Flame.

"It sounds to me like an escaped Lay Reader," said her Host.

With a single impulse they both started for the door.

"Don't worry, Little Girl," whispered the young Stranger in the dark hall.

"I'll try not to," quivered Flame.

They were both right, it seemed.

It was Parents *and* the Lay Reader.

All three breathless, all three excited, all three reproachful,--they swept into the warm, balsam-scented Rattle-Pane House with a gust of frost, a threat of disaster.

**KARTINDO PUBLISING HOUSE (Kartindo.com)**

"F--lame," sighed her Father.

"Flame!" scolded her Mother.

"Flame?" implored the Lay Reader.

"What a pretty name," beamed the Master of the House. "Pray be seated, everybody," he gestured graciously to left and right,--shoving one dog expeditiously under the table with his foot, while he yanked another out of a chair with his least gesticulating hand. "This is certainly a very great pleasure, I assure you," he affirmed distinctly to Miss Flamande Nourice. "Returning quite unexpectedly to my new house this lonely Christmas evening," he explained very definitely to the Rev. Flamande Nourice, "I can't express to you what it means to me to find this pleasant gathering of neighbors waiting here to welcome me! And when I think of the effort *you* must have made to get here, Mr. Bertrand," he beamed. "A young man of all your obligations and--complications--"

"Pleasant ... gathering of neighbors?" questioned Mrs. Nourice with some emotion.

"Oh, I forgot," deprecated the Master of the House with real concern. "Your Christmas season is not, of course, as inherently 'pleasant' as one might wish.... I was told at the railroad station how you and Mr. Nourice had been called away by the illness of a relative."

"We were called away," confided Mrs. Nourice with increasing asperity, "called away at considerable inconvenience--by a very sick relative--to receive the present of a Piebald pony."

"Oh, goody!" quickened Flame and collapsed again under the weight of her Mother's glance.

"And then came this terrible telephone message," shuddered her Mother. "The implied dishonor of one of your Father's most trusted--most trusted associates!"

"I was right in the midst of such an interesting book," deplored her Father. "And Uncle Wally wouldn't lend it."

"So we borrowed Uncle Wally's new automobile and started right for home!" explained her Mother. "It was at the Junction that we made connections with the Constable and his prisoner."

"His--victim," intercepted the Lay Reader coldly.

At this interception everybody turned suddenly and looked at the Lay Reader. His mouth was twisted very slightly to one side. It gave him a rather unpleasant snarling expression. If this expression had been vocal instead of muscular it would have shocked his hearers.

"Your Father had to go on board the train and identify him," persisted Flame's Mother. "It was very distressing.... The Constable was most unwilling to release him. Your Father had to use every kind of an argument."

"Every ... kind," mused her Father. "He doesn't even deny being in the house," continued her Mother, "being in my closet, ... being caught with a--a--"

"With a silver carving knife and fork in his hand," intercepted the Lay Reader hastily.

"Yet all the time he persists," frowned Flame's Mother, "that there is some one in the world who can give a perfectly good explanation if only,--he won't even say 'he or she' but 'it', if only 'it' would."

Something in the stricken expression of her daughter's face brought a sudden flicker of suspicion to the Mother's eyes.

"*You* don't know anything about this, do you, Flame?" she demanded. "Is it remotely possible that after your promise to me,--your sacred promise to me--?" The whole structure of the home,--of mutual confidence,--of all the Future itself, crackled and toppled in her voice.

To the Lay Reader's face, and right *through* the Lay Reader's face, to the face of the Master of the House, Flame's glance went homing with an unaccountable impulse.

With one elbow leaning casually on the mantle-piece, his narrowed eyes faintly inscrutable, faintly smiling, it seemed suddenly to the young Master of the House that he had been waiting all his discouraged years for just that glance. His heart gave the queerest jump.

Flame's face turned suddenly very pink.

Like a person in a dream, she turned back to her Mother. There was a smile on her face, but even the smile was the smile of a dreaming person.

"No--Mother," she said, "I haven't seen Bertrand ... to-day."

"Why, you're looking right at him now!" protested her exasperated Mother.

With a gentle murmur of dissent, Flame's Father stepped forward and laid his arm across the young girl's shoulder. "She--she may be looking at him," he said. "But I'm almost perfectly sure that she doesn't ... see him."

"Why, whatever in the world do you mean?" demanded his wife. "Whatever in the world does anybody mean? If there was only another woman here! A mature ... sane woman! A----" With a flare of accusation she turned from Flame to the Master of the House. "This Miss Flora that my daughter spoke of,--where is she? I insist on seeing her! Please summon her instantly!"

Crossing genially to the table the Master of the House reached down and dragged out the Bull Dog by the brindled scuff of her neck. The scratch on her nose was still bleeding slightly. And one eye was closed.

"This is--Miss Flora!" he said.

Indignantly Flame's Mother glanced at the dog, and then from her daughter's face to the face of the young man again.

"And you call *that*--a lady?" she demanded.

"N--not technically," admitted the young man.

For an instant a perfectly tense silence reigned. Then from under a shadowy basket the Cat crept out, shining, sinuous, with extended paw, and began to pat a sprig of holly cautiously along the floor.

Yielding to the reaction Flame bent down suddenly and hugging the Wolf Hound's head to her breast buried her face in the soft, sweet shagginess.

"Not sanitary, Mother?" she protested. "Why, they're as sanitary as--as violets!"

As though dreaming he were late to church and had forgotten his vestments, Flame's Father reached out nervously and draped a great string of ground-pine stole-like about his neck.

"We all," broke in the Master of the House quite irrelevantly, "seem to have experienced a slight twinge of irritability--the past few minutes. Hunger, I've no doubt!... So suppose we all sit down together to this sumptuous--if somewhat chilled repast? After the soup certainly, even after very cold soup, all explanations I'm sure will be--cheerfully and satisfactorily exchanged. Miss-- Flame I know has a most amusing story to tell and--"

"Oh, yes!" rallied Flame. "And it's almost all about being blindfolded and sending poor Mr. Lorello--"

"So if by any chance, Mr.--Mr. Bertrand," interrupted the Master of the House a bit abruptly, "you happen to have the carving knife and fork still on your person ... I thought I saw a white string hanging--"

"I have!" said the Lay Reader with his first real grin.

With great formality the Master of the House drew back a chair and bowed Flame's Mother to it.

Then suddenly the Red Setter lifted his sensitive nose in the air, and the spotted Dalmatian bristled faintly across the ridge of his back. Through the whole room, it seemed, swept a curious cottony sense of Something-About-to- Happen! Was it that a sound hushed? Or that a hush decided suddenly to be a sound?

With a little sharp catch of her breath Flame dashed to the window, and swung the sash upward! Where once had breathed the drab, dusty smell of frozen grass and mud quickened suddenly a curious metallic dampness like the smell of new pennies.

"Mr. ... Delcote!" she called.

In an instant his slender form silhouetted darkly with hers in the open window against the eternal mystery and majesty of a Christmas night.

"And *then* the snow came!"

## THE END

**KARTINDO PUBLISING HOUSE (Kartindo.com)**

www.ingramcontent.com/pod-product-compliance
Lightning Source LLC
Chambersburg PA
CBHW070341290526
45791CB00003B/1425